NATIONAL
GEOGRAPH

Storms

Andrew Collins

Contents

Violent Weather

Air is all around us. We can't see it, but we can feel it when it blows. When the wind blows, air from somewhere else moves in. The new air might be warmer or cooler, drier or wetter. When two bodies of air collide, or crash into each other, **storms** develop. Storms are periods of violent weather.

Thunderstorms

It's a warm summer day. Late in the afternoon the sky turns dark. The wind starts to blow. The temperature drops. A bright light flashes across the sky. A thundering crash booms. Soon rain will pour from the sky. A thunderstorm is near.

Thunderstorms are storms that produce **lightning** and **thunder**. They often cause heavy rain and strong winds. Thunderstorms are the most common of all severe, or violent, storms. Luckily, thunderstorms don't usually last a long time. Most are over within an hour or two.

Why Thunderstorms Form

Thunderstorms form when a body of cold air high in the sky crashes into warm, moist air that is low to the ground. The warm air moves upward and the two types of air mix. Huge, dark, anvil-shaped clouds form. They bring lightning, thunder, and heavy rain.

Water droplets at the top of the cloud begin to fall.

Warm, moist air rises.

Thunder and Lightning

Thunder is loud, but it can't hurt you. Lightning can. A lightning bolt is a giant spark of **electricity**. As the air mixes within a storm cloud, electricity builds up. When enough electricity builds up, a giant spark of lightning results.

When lightning flashes, a great amount of heat is released. The heat warms the air, causing it to **expand** with an explosion. The expanding air creates the thunder we hear.

Thunderstorm Damage

Thunderstorms can be dangerous. Strong winds can knock down trees and power lines. Heavy rains can cause **flooding**. Every year lightning kills about 100 people in the United States.

Staying Safe

You can stay safe during a thunderstorm if you follow these safety tips when a storm develops.

If you are inside

- Stay indoors.

- Don't use the telephone or electrical equipment such as a computer or a television.

- Stay out of the bathtub or shower.

If you are outside

- Seek shelter.

- Get out of the water and small boats.

- If you can't go inside, find a low spot away from trees or poles. Squat down and cover your head. Don't lie on the ground.

Tornadoes

Severe thunderstorms have replaced the calm of a sunny summer afternoon. As the thunderstorms pass through, the wind grows stronger and stronger. The sound of the wind becomes so loud it is almost deafening. It sounds as though several jet airplanes are taking off at once. Dirt flies through the air. A tornado is coming.

A **tornado** is a funnel-shaped column of strong wind that stretches from a storm cloud to the ground. Tornadoes are the most violent of all storms. The winds in the strongest tornadoes can spin at more than 300 miles (480 kilometers) per hour. Tornadoes are sometimes called twisters because of their strong, spinning winds.

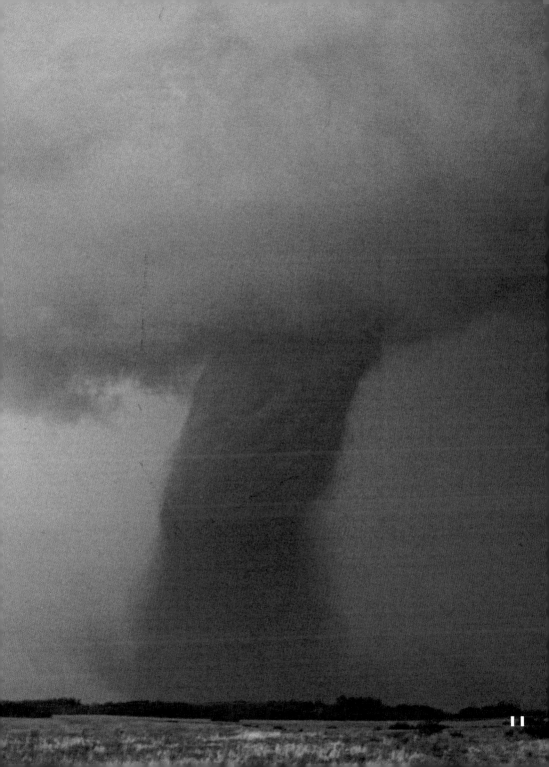

Why Tornadoes Form

Tornadoes form when the cool air of a storm cloud settles on top of warm air and traps it. When some of the warm air breaks through the cool air, it spirals, or spins, upward. This creates the swirling wind of a funnel cloud.

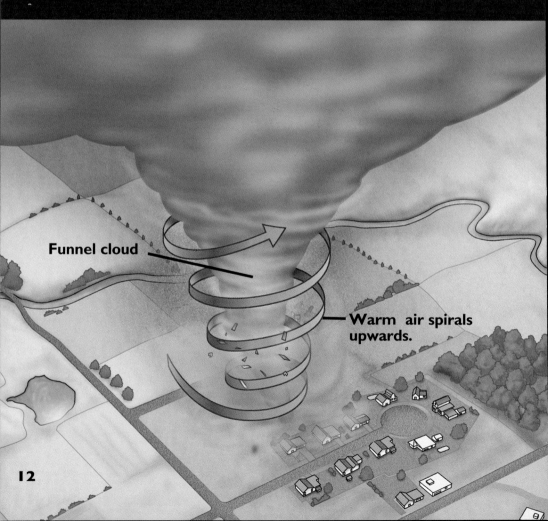

Funnel cloud

Warm air spirals upwards.

A tornado's funnel cloud acts like a giant vacuum cleaner. When it touches the ground, it picks up everything in its path—trees, cars, even the roofs off houses. A funnel cloud looks dark because of all the dirt and trash flying around in the spinning wind.

Tornado Damage

Most tornadoes last less than 15 minutes, but they can be deadly. A powerful twister can tear a house apart and throw the pieces in all directions.

Tornadoes can occur anywhere in the world, but more tornadoes form in the United States than any other country. The central part of the country—from north Texas to Iowa—is known as Tornado Alley. Hundreds of tornadoes occur here each year.

Tornado Alley

Tornadoes are most likely to occur in places shown in orange.

14

Staying Safe

The national weather service warns us when there are severe storms. The best way to stay safe is to pay attention to these warnings.

A **tornado watch** means weather conditions are right for a tornado to form. Stay alert to warnings and be prepared to take shelter.

A **tornado warning** means a tornado has been seen in the area. If you hear a **tornado warning**, take shelter.

- Go to the basement or lowest level of your house. Crouch under the stairs or heavy furniture. Cover your head.

- If you can't go inside, lie down in a ditch or other low area. Get out of cars.

Hurricanes

Howling winds bend the trees nearly to the ground. Heavy rain pours from the sky. People have boarded up their windows. They are heading inland until the storm passes. A hurricane is heading towards shore.

A **hurricane** is a huge, swirling storm that forms over warm ocean waters. Hurricanes are the largest and most destructive of all storms. They can measure 500 miles (800 kilometers) across and can cause high winds and heavy rain as far as 250 miles (400 kilometers) away.

Why Hurricanes Form

Hurricanes form when a group of thunderstorms come together over a warm sea to form a large storm. The storm clouds spin together in a circle. The sea provides the storm with **energy** and moisture. It becomes bigger and stronger. At the center of the storm is a calm area called the "eye." The clouds spin around the eye very quickly. When the winds in the spinning storm reach 74 miles (119 kilometers) per hour, the storm is called a hurricane.

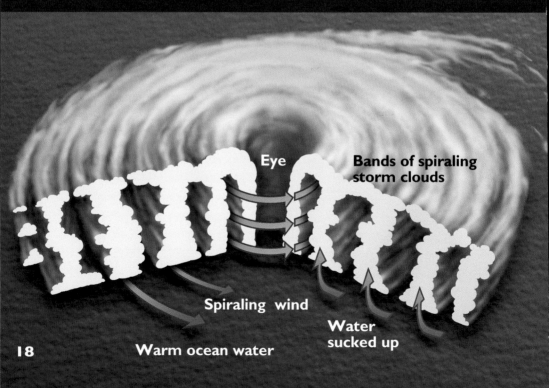

Eye

Bands of spiraling storm clouds

Spiraling wind

Water sucked up

Warm ocean water

This picture of a hurricane was taken from space.

As the hurricane moves across the ocean, a wall of seawater called a **storm surge** forms under the storm. This huge wave can cause a lot of damage when it hits the coast.

Hurricane Damage

When hurricanes move over land, they destroy most things in their path. As scary as the winds are, most hurricane damage is caused by flooding from heavy rains and huge waves. Roads, houses, and cars can be swept away. In 1991 a hurricane killed 135,000 people in Asia.

Hurricanes are called different things in different parts of the world. These storms are called typhoons when they form in the western Pacific Ocean. They are called cyclones in Australia and countries around the Indian Ocean.

Hurricanes form in the parts of the ocean shown in yellow. Arrows show the direction they travel.

Staying Safe

The weather service tracks hurricanes and predicts when and where they will come ashore. They warn people when it's not safe to stay along the coast. The best way to stay safe is to follow these warnings.

A **hurricane watch** means a hurricane is possible within 36 hours. Stay alert to warnings and gather items for a disaster supply kit:

- Food and water for two weeks

- Flashlight and batteries

- Change of clothing and blankets

- Portable radio

- First aid kit

A **hurricane warning** means a hurricane is expected within 24 hours. You may be asked to evacuate, or leave your home. If you're not asked to evacuate, stay inside until the storm has passed.

Weather Watch

Predicting and tracking storms is a big job. **Meteorologists** are scientists who study the weather. They use **satellites**, weather balloons, and other tools to gather information about changing weather conditions. They use this information to make predictions about when and where storms will form. Their predictions can help keep us safe from dangerous storms.

Glossary

electricity	a form of energy
energy	power or strength
expand	to get bigger
flooding	the flow of water over normally dry land
hurricane	a huge, swirling storm that forms over ocean waters
lightning	a flash of light caused by a giant spark of electricity in a storm cloud
meteorologist	a person who studies the weather
satellite	a machine that orbits the Earth, recording weather conditions on Earth
storm	a period of violent weather
storm surge	a huge wave that forms beneath a hurricane
thunder	the noise heard after lightning flashes
thunderstorm	a storm that produces lightning and thunder
tornado	a funnel-shaped column of spinning wind

Index